T0276810

ANOTHER WORLD:
LOSING OUR CHILDREN
TO ISLAMIC STATE

Gillian Slovo

ANOTHER WORLD:
LOSING OUR CHILDREN
TO ISLAMIC STATE

based on verbatim interviews
developed with Nicolas Kent from his original idea

OBERON BOOKS
LONDON

WWW.OBERONBOOKS.COM

First published in 2016 by Oberon Books Ltd
521 Caledonian Road, London N7 9RH
Tel: +44 (0) 20 7607 3637 / Fax: +44 (0) 20 7607 3629
e-mail: info@oberonbooks.com
www.oberonbooks.com

Copyright © Gillian Slovo, 2016

Gillian Slovo is hereby identified as author of this play
in accordance with section 77 of the Copyright, Designs and
Patents Act 1988. The author has asserted her moral rights.

All rights whatsoever in this play are strictly reserved and
application for performance etc. should be made before
commencement of rehearsal to United Agents, 12-26 Lexington
Street, London W1F 0LE (info@unitedagents.co.uk). No
performance may be given unless a licence has been obtained,
and no alterations may be made in the title or the text of the play
without the author's prior written consent.

You may not copy, store, distribute, transmit, reproduce or
otherwise make available this publication (or any part of it) in
any form, or binding or by any means (print, electronic, digital,
optical, mechanical, photocopying, recording or otherwise),
without the prior written permission of the publisher. Any person
who does any unauthorized act in relation to this publication may
be liable to criminal prosecution and civil claims for damages.

A catalogue record for this book is available from the British
Library.

PB ISBN: 9781783197552
E ISBN: 9781783197569

Cover image by Getty Images

Visit www.oberonbooks.com to read more about all our books
and to buy them. You will also find features, author interviews and
news of any author events, and you can sign up for e-newsletters
so that you're always first to hear about our new releases.

Another World: Losing Our Children to Islamic State

written by Gillian Slovo
developed with Nicolas Kent from his original idea

CAST, in order of speaking

Abu Bakr Al-Baghdadi / Mohammed Akunjee **NABIL ELOUAHABI**
Yasmin **NATHALIE ARMIN**
Geraldine / Assistant Commissioner Helen Ball **PENNY LAYDEN**
Zarlasht Halamzai / Female Student **LARA SAWALHA**
Moazzam Begg / Tufyal Choudhury **PHALDUT SHARMA**
Shiraz Mahir **GARY PILLAI**
Samira **SIRINE SABA**
Charlie Winter **GUNNAR CAUTHERY**
General John Allen / Charles Farr **JACK ELLIS**
Male Student **FARSHID ROKEY**
Male Student **RONAK PATANI**
Female Student **ZARA AZAM**
Reverend Doctor Paul Fitzpatrick **TIM WOODWARD**

Director **Nicolas Kent**
Designer **Lucy Sierra**
Video Designer **Duncan McLean**
Lighting Designer **Matthew Eagland**
Sound Designer **Mike Winship**
Dialect Coach **Majella Hurley**
Assistant Director **Kwami Odoom**

Casting **Charlotte Bevan**
Production Photographer **Tristram Kenton**

WORLD PREMIERE

National Theatre's temporary theatre, 15 April 2016

LENGTH

About 95 minutes. There will be no interval.

The National Theatre is dedicated to making the very best theatre and sharing it with as many people as possible.

We stage up to 30 productions at our South Bank home each year, ranging from re-imagined classics – such as Greek tragedy and Shakespeare – to modern masterpieces and new work by contemporary writers and theatre-makers. The work we make strives to be as open, as diverse, as collaborative and as national as possible. Much of that new work is researched and developed at the NT Studio: we are committed to nurturing innovative work from new writers, directors, creative artists and performers. Equally, we are committed to education, with a wide-ranging Learning programme for all ages in the new Clore Learning Centre and in schools and communities across the UK.

The National's work is also seen on tour throughout the UK and internationally, and in collaborations and co-productions with regional theatres. Popular shows transfer to the West End and occasionally to Broadway; and through the National Theatre Live programme, we broadcast live performances to 2,000 cinemas in 50 countries around the world. From 2015, *National Theatre: On Demand in Schools* made acclaimed, curriculum-linked productions free to stream on demand in every secondary school in the country. Online, the NT offers a rich variety of innovative digital content on every aspect of theatre.

We do all we can to keep ticket prices affordable and to reach a wide audience, and use our public funding to maintain artistic risk-taking, accessibility and diversity.

nationaltheatre.org.uk

Director of the National Theatre **Rufus Norris**
Executive Director **Lisa Burger**

Another World was the dream child of Nicolas Kent who came to me, as he had done twice before, with a proposal to collaborate on a play about Islamic State. As terrifying as that sounded, I have learned to trust Nicolas's proposals, and knew that he would be by my side every step of the way during the realisation of this project. And so it proved. A very special thanks to him.

I interviewed many people in the process of compiling the play and then had the difficult task of choosing whose words should run through the play. I couldn't put everybody I talked to in, but every interview helped me understand the complicated terrain in which we nowadays dwell. My thanks to those I interviewed, and those who helped in other ways: Sohail Ahmed, Mohamed Akunjee, Rashad Ali, General John Allen,David Anderson, DAC Helen Ball, Moazzam Begg, Mia Bloom, Christina Blower, Moad el'Boundati, Mia Bloom, Katherine Brown, Jason Burke, Tufyal Choudhury, Isis du Blois, Peter Fahy, Charles Farr, Reverend Paul Fitzpatrick, Matt Foot, Zarlasht Halamzai, Abdul Haqq, Usama Hasan, Sacha Havilcek, Duncan James, Na'eem Jeneh, Sophia Jouahri, Alyas Karmani, Imran Khan, Hugo Macpherson, Michael Macy, Gaelle Mechine, Cassie Metcalf-Slovo, Ibrahim Mohamoud, Shiraz Mahir, Tilly O'Neill, Richard Norton-Taylor, Hanif Qadir, Lord Richards of Herstmonceux, Mark Sedwill, Rizwaan Sabir, Vanessa September, Edit Schlaffer, Kamila Shamsie, Jessika Soors, Clive Stafford Smith, the workers of Travailleurs du Rue, Brussels, Kiri Tunks, Asim Qureshi, Huma Yusuf, Sacha Wares and Charlie Winter.

Thanks to Anita Nayyaar whose work on our behalf made a radical difference to the project and thank you as well to the wonderful staff of the National Theatre particularly Ben Power, Sarah J Murray, Rufus Norris and Bernie Whittle. Thanks also to the sixth formers from Tower Hamlets who I talked to twice and who asked to remain anonymous. And finally thanks to the mothers Chantal, Geraldine, Samira, Saida, Saliha and Yasmin who, despite their pain, were generous in sharing their stories with us. (some of their names have been changed at their request).

I have edited the interviews always paying attention to keeping the sense of what each person said. Any words or phrases that I added are in square brackets.

Gillian Slovo

Characters in order of appearance

Abu Bakr al-Baghdadi: Islamic State Caliph

Geraldine: a Belgian mother

Yasmin: a Belgian mother

Zarlasht Halaimzai: Afghan born. An education in emergencies advisor

Moazzam Begg: British Muslim imprisoned from 2002-2005 at Bagram and Guantanamo without charge or trial. Since his release he has been campaigning against War on Terror abuses as outreach director for advocacy group CAGE.

Shiraz Maher: Senior Research Fellow for the International Centre for the Study of Radicalisation at Kings College

Samira: a Belgian mother

General John Allen: Four star Marine Corps general who served President Obama's special envoy to the global coalition to counter ISIL Aug 2014 until 12th November, 2015. Presently retired but still advising the Secretary of State on matters relating to ISIL.

Charlie Winter: Senior Research Associate at Georgia State University's Transcultural Conflict and Violence Initiative.

four anonymous six form school students – A. B. C and D – from a school in Tower Hamlets

Mohammed Akunjee: Solicitor who deals with terrorism or extreme Muslim related matters (solicitor to the three Bethnal Green families)

Reverend Doctor Paul Fitzpatrick: Chaplain and Researcher into radicalisation and grooming in Cardiff Metropolitan University

DAC Helen Ball: Deputy Assistant Commissioner within the Metropolitan Police and Senior National Coordinator Counter Terrorism Policing

David Cameron: British Prime Minister

Charles Farr: former Director General of the Office of Security and Counterterrorism and current Chair of the Joint Intelligence Committee

Tufyal Choudhury: Durham university law lecturer and researcher into the impact of counterterrorism measures on Muslim communities in the UK

On a screen the words: Raqqa 2013

The black ISIS logo runs down the screen to sound of water [Eid 2013 video] and goes to black

Footage of Abu Bakr al Baghdadi mounting a lectern in a mosque

Text on screen:

A message to the Mujadhadin and the Muslim Ummah in the month of Ramadan by the Caliph Abu Bakr al-Baghdadi

In Arabic [for the first line] which fades for the English delivered on stage by an actor:

Raise your head high, for today – by Allah's grace – you have a state and caliphate.

It is a state where the Arab and non-Arab, the white man and black man, the Easterner and Westerner are all brothers. Their blood mixed and became one, under a single flag and goal, in one pavilion.

Therefore, rush, o Muslims, to your state. Rush, because Syria is not for the Syrians, and Iraq is not for the Iraqis. The Earth is Allah's.

Now on screen we see a section from ISIS's 2013 Eid Video:

Men in a mosque in Raqqa rising to their feet, arms outstretched shouting:

Takbir! Allahu Akbar!

The Islamic State ... will remain!

Takbir! Allahu Akbar!

As the congregation disperses the video shows men hugging each other, music[1] comes up along with images [cut to include young boy with huge gun]

fade music before the end

on the video comes a card:

Eid Greetings form the Land of Khilafah

which changes to a man on screen, his name:

Abu Abdulla al-Habashi from Britain

speaking to camera:

I'm from the UK, my name's Abu Abdullah Al-Habashi. Er, today is – er – it's Eid

the music continues against Abu Abdullah Al-Habashi on a horse on screen

Then him speaking to camera

Abu Abdullah Al-Habashi

Iandsa Khalifa, Allahu Akbhar Iandsa Khalifa. I don't think there's anything better than living in the land of Khilafah, the, you know the, the the the rights and the, you know, you're not living under oppression, you're not living under Zulm you know, you're not living under kufar. And hamdullah you're living you're living by the Qu'ran and you're living by the Sunnah. And really and truly as as Muslims that's all we want and that's that's all we need. We don't need any democracy, we don't need any communism, we don't need anything like that, all we need is Sharia.

fade to black [end video]

Now on screen the words: Molenbeek, Brussels October 2015

---

[1] *The Shari'ah of our Lord is light, by it we rise over the stars.*
By it we live without humiliation, a life of peace and security.
The Shari'ah of our Lord is light, by it we rise over the stars.
By it we live without humiliation, a life of peace and security

Two mothers Yasmin and Geraldine on stage

Yasmin (mother of Karim who went to Syria)

[My son is] Karim. He's 20 now. He turned 20 on 22nd January [2015].

He was in 6th year getting a technical qualification, learning to be an electrician. He had problems with one of the teachers: she was always on his case. For instance she would ask him questions but only him: about homosexuality ... what did he think about it? Or erh ... about terrorism, what he thought, about the *Charlie Hebdo* attacks. She always picked on him.

He was called to the headmaster's office. He spoke to the Head respectfully. He said: I don't agree with homosexuality. Erh, for me, God created man and woman for a reason, but I respect them erh ... about ... about of the *Charlie Hebdo* attacks, he did say that ... that, that religions, you can't talk about it ... that you have to ... it's ... it's sacred, that you can't talk about it, but that he's against violence. And erh, on the subject of terrorism, well he was against it. He said, he said to the Head: look at what I'm like. He's a young guy who smoked, who went out clubbing, who ... I'm not saying that's good but come on, that's what people do.

Geraldine (mother of Anis who went to Syria)

I'm Muslim, I converted 23 years ago. My husband is of Moroccan origin.

My son was 18. He spoke French, Dutch, English, he spoke Arabic, he knew Italian, so that would normally be a plus point for finding work. But the problem, you have to remember that here in Brussels, and I think it's a bit like this all over Belgium, there is still discrimination. It, it will always be there. I work in Human Resources, and I know that my colleagues say: I'd never employ a Pakistani, an Arab, a Romanian, a Turk, never. *(Pause.)* But these children were born here in Belgium. They are Belgian, right? It's just that their faces are a little bit more tanned.

Yasmin

They don't have the right first name, the right surname, the right look. But they're not ugly, they're not stupid, and still they're never given a chance ... At every street corner [Karim] would get checked by the police. Even though they knew very well he was from around here he would get checked.

Geraldine

My son couldn't find work. So he said to me: Mum, I don't know what I'm doing here. In inverted commas, but just like that. I don't know what I'm doing here on Earth. Because when I'm in Belgium, I'm Moroccan, but when we go on holiday to Morocco, well I, I'm Belgian, and people don't accept me. Where am I going to work? Where can I make my home?

So he started to go to the library, and at the same time, his discourse began to change. He would say to us: have you seen what's happening in Palestine? I said: yes, but Palestine's been that way for more than 60 years: we can't intervene. Yes, but it's not normal. Everyday there are Palestinians being killed! And we're not doing anything. And then later, bit by bit, since he saw that in fact we weren't reacting, he came to us with the problem of Syria. He said to us: yes in Syria Muslims are being massacred every day by Bashar, and I'm a Muslim, I have to do something. Even my government has said – because it's true that to begin with Belgium said Bashar couldn't do that and we, Belgium, are against Bashar – even my government agrees with me, we have to do something against Bashar.

Yasmin

It was half term and [Karim had] booked tickets to go to Morocco with a friend, to go to his friend's family, for a week, I mean why not? *(Tears in voice.)* On the 14th February, I was meeting my daughter *(pause)* at a restaurant with her brother too *(tears in voice)* so we could be together as a family ... so erh ... *(her voice trembles)* he doesn't come. I phone him. I say: Karim where are you? We're waiting for you! He says to me: Mum, it's no big deal, eat, I'm with a friend. *(We can still hear the emotion in her voice.)* I was like: come, you go to Morocco tomorrow. Come ... you'll see your sister, before she's operated on on Monday. He says:

let me speak to my sister. Then he speaks to his sister, he says: I hope you get better and, well, may God be with you and well, I'm leaving. She says: have a safe journey, and everything *(someone brings her a glass of water)* I'll be fine, thank you – have a safe trip and everything. I go home, I wait. *(Sobbing.)*

Geraldine

[My son] said to me: Mum, I'm going to go to Syria. Whether Dad agrees or not, I'm going to go to Syria. We tried to tell him in every way possible not to go. I ... I made him see people from the main mosque who had been there, who had come back and who said to him: no, you mustn't go over there. We can't do anything, it's a political war, we can't intervene. But my son didn't want to listen. For him, the Imams were *bisounours*, like Care Bears [they're weak and soft] and and they work for the state, so I don't want to listen to the Belgian Imams anymore. We didn't know that that was already the line the recruiters were using with him.

He said to me: Mum, I'm leaving on 22nd January.

My husband and I, we thought, right, we'll go to the police, it was Sunday night. After waiting for two hours, two policemen came and they recorded our report, but we could see that they were following questions that they had probably found from another hearing or from a set list they had been given. So we explained everything what we knew, and [one] said to us: listen, what I'm going to do is I'm going to put a ... a note, a note on the file saying that your son might be part of a terrorist group, that way he won't get on the plane.

The 22nd January comes round and I get a phone call but I can't see the number. I thought it was my son who was going to ring me up saying: Mum, what have you done? Or something. But no, it was a Turkish telephone number in fact, ringing me up and telling me: Madam, are you Anis's mother? I say: yes. Well you can ring this number in two hours. He's in Turkey. He's going to Syria.

Me, straight away, I phone the [police] inspector, because he gave us his number, and I say to him: my son's gone. And he says to me: no, that's not possible. I say to him: yes, he's gone.

Yasmin

Karim comes home really late. I get angry, I say to him: listen you're going on holiday, you should've been with with us. He says to me: it isn't a big deal, mum, I had to lend my friend a hand ... I say: ok. [But] I see his eyes are all red. I go: what's going on? *(Worried.)* What's up? He says to me: nothing, I haven't slept, that's all. *(Silence.)* I ... *(Tears in voice.)* I ask him how many kilos he's allowed to take on holiday. He says: 20 kilos. I go: are you sure? He goes to me: Yes, I think it's 20 kilos. I go: show me your ticket and he says to me: no, they're, it isn't, it's at my friend's. I go: ok.

Normally I look at it. Normally I go with him. And that day I don't know what happened. I didn't look, I didn't go with him *(Pause.)* He didn't say goodbye. I mean, he didn't kiss his brother, his brother's wife, he took me in his arms *(she's crying)*, he squeezed me tight and he left.

Three days later, [Karim] phones me, he's on the beach in Tangiers and he says: it's sunny. I go: be, be careful you don't get married in Morocco.

[The next day] I go to my mum's house. I don't know anything at that point. And my children come, my sister-in-law was there, and I don't notice anything. Then I start to talk to my boys, and my eldest son goes into the kitchen, and my mum gets angry, and then my daughter comes in. And then, I knew that something was up. I go: what's wrong with you? She goes: nothing. But what's up with you? I thought it was one of her children who had a problem. She goes: Mum, it's, Karim: he's gone. What's happened to him? She says to me, he's gone. I go: he's dead She says: he's gone to Syria.

He had phoned his brother telling him that he had entered the land of Shâm and that he didn't want to come back here *(Crying.)* That he didn't belong here anymore ... *(crying)* in this country.

I heard this word, Syria, Syria. I felt the world fall on top of me. I didn't see it coming I haven't done my job as a mother properly. I'll never see him again, I didn't get to kiss him, tell him that I loved him, that he was everything to me.

Geraldine

I telephoned my son in the evening, and he said to me: but Mum, don't worry. I came here, it's to help the Muslims. I'm going to live in Muslim territory. So it was a refrain every time I called him right: I'm going to live in Muslim territory, where I can practice my religion, and, how shall I put it, where things are governed by Sharia law. And if I die, well then I'll be opening the doors to Paradise for you.

fade up the sound of the Eid music

On screen: July 1, 2014 as backing to Abu Bakr Al-Baghadadi

Abu Bakr Al-Baghdadi

The Muslims were defeated after the fall of their khilafa. Then their state ceased to exist, so the disbelievers were able to weaken and humiliate the Muslims, dominate them in every region, plunder their wealth and resources, and rob them of their rights.

Those rulers continue striving to enslave the Muslims, pulling them away from their religion.

Zarlasht Halaimzai (an education in emergencies advisor)

I grew up in the '80s in Afghanistan – I can see where this beast has evolved from. But if you talk to people here, there seems to be this mystery about radicalisation and global jihad: Is it about Islam? Is it about Muslims? And it's, it's, it's really odd. It's, it's almost like wilful blindness about history.

Global jihad comes from the Cold War era um, the policies that were implemented in Afghanistan, um, and other Muslim [countries]. That was about opposing the USSR, and particularly in Afghanistan, the Americans sought out, with the help of ISI, which is the Pakistan intelligence service, to find extreme Islamist groups [and] train them. There are allegations that Osama bin Laden was supported by the CIA. He was certainly operating at this time and he ran with this idea that you, as a Muslim, you have to wage jihad on behalf of Muslims everywhere. It's not an idea that had been used beforehand. So in Afghanistan, when the British invaded in the 19th century, people declared jihad because a foreign invader had come into Afghanistan, and it was about expelling foreign invaders from [the] country. It was a very national affair. But during the Cold War, with the help of Saudis, the Pakistani

Government, Americans, British, this idea was cultivated that as a Muslim, you are supposed to go and wage jihad on behalf of any Muslim nations in the world.

Moazzam Begg

I [joined] up with the foreign volunteer force which was a, a wing of the Bosnian Army [in the early 1990s]. I stayed with them for a, for a few weeks. I didn't see any action, but I was with the fighters and I did see lots of wounded people and I did attend the fronts, and the hospitals, and um ... see people from all over the world taking part in this conflict of defence. And, and I remember very clearly, because around this time [the massacre at] Srebrenica had happened, and [the massacre at] Gorazde had happened. And this was the sort of ... factor that moved me, and I believe many others, into believing that sometimes you have to take drastic steps. In order to prevent a greater catastrophe. And, and that's I think coupled with the search for identity for me, was crucial.

Shiraz Maher (senior Research Fellow at the International Centre for the Study of Radicalization at Kings College London)

Prior to September the 11th, I was probably someone who would describe himself as an atheist, um, but someone who was deeply interested in politics. I'd grown up in Saudi Arabia [but] I didn't particularly have a great degree of fondness for [it]. So, at that point I'm living a very typical first year undergraduate university experience [at Leeds university], by which I mean I'm trying to drink as much as possible, trying to get laid as much as possible, smoking weed fairly regularly [but I'm also] definitely thinking a lot more about identity.

Then September 11th happens and my basic attitude is not one of immediate revulsion but is a sense of, well, you deserve this. The United States has, ah, if I can be blunt, fucked with the Muslim world. It has been a malignant force for Islam and in the Muslim world and therefore, you know, 9/11 is legitimate payback. It's blood back.

I go to the mosque. The community's scared. People don't wanna talk about it. And here you have these guys from Hisb ut-Tahrir who [are] defiant, they're bold, they're confident but they also seem to me like they're winners. The guy who recruited me said, come to my house. I go there and I, I remember it vividly, we put on the news. There was still smoke coming from the twin towers, from that smouldering wreck.

He says, so what do you make about this? So, I said, well, you know, I don't think Islam can justify this [but] I'm here to ask you, what do you think, and he says, well, you know, it's an irrelevance now because it's happened. What really matters is that the United States is gonna use this as a pretext to prosecute a war on Islam. So, I'm like, oh, yeah, America's always been at war with Islam. We have a duty not just to Islam but to look after our interests and, you know, George Bush is there saying you're either with us or against us and I'm saying, I'm not with you, and if the world is a binary, then I am afraid I have to be on the other side.

At a basic human level, you do understand there's a tragedy and you do empathise at that personal level but we have 9/11s every day – that was my thinking. So, just cos it happened to white bankers who are, you know, living in downtown Manhattan ... You know, the Afghan tribes love their children just as much as he loves his wife or his kids. So, I said to Hisb ut-Tahrir, I want in. I wanna be part of the great Islamic revolution that is coming. We will change the world and right it.

I became really a Party man I [was living in] a house with non-Muslims, with all my buddies, obviously, but Hisb ut-Tahrir said, you can't live with non-Muslims. So, I moved into a house just with other, with other Muslims, ultimately with other members of Hisb ut-Tahrir. I lived directly opposite from the mosque. You know, we were not just waking up to those prayers, we were going to the mosque for those prayers. I had one of those zebibahs. It's sort of tough and hard and calloused skin on your forehead from prostrating all day. We really went for it.

17

fade up the Eid music

Abu Bakr- al Baghdadi

Soon, by Allah's permission, a day will come when the Muslim will walk everywhere as a master, having honor, being revered, with his head raised high and his dignity preserved.

Samira (mother of Nora who went to Syria)

My daughter was a completely ordinary girl. Like any other girl you might find in the world in any country. A girl who loved fashion, who loved her friends, her school, makeup. [But] she was always looking for something.

Around ... around 16, she starts telling me that she feels useless. She says, Yes, I'd really like to ... have a goal in my life. But afterwards, she got over that phase and she kept went to school and everything. [Then] one day she says to me, Mum ... I'd want to ... wear a hijab, wear a veil and everything. And I explain to her, I say to her, Nora, listen, you know ... it's very difficult to find work, make a life for yourself if you wear a veil, if you dress in a hijab and everything else. I say, Look at me for starters, me. I don't wear a veil, I'm divorced and that's difficult enough. I have a job but it's hard. I say, Have a think ... Keep going to school, think, and if at the end of the year you still ... you still want to, we'll see.

So she kept going to school as normal and everything and then one day at the end of the year, she comes downstairs wearing a full veil. And I see her and I say, Ahhh, and she says, Yes, you told me, she says, I want to wear this. And of course because I'm Muslim myself I say, There's nothing wrong with it. You see, if she's chosen to wear it, if it makes her happy ... if she wants to wear ... ...

But after I knew the full story ... ... in fact these young girls, my daughter, everything was already planned.

[The headmaster gave her permission to wear the veil and everything but one day] she says to me, Yes, but they don't accept me for who I am. They are angry at me because I wear a veil. She says I don't want to go to school anymore and in September I will find somewhere to live, some work, I will do a course so I can work with children. She liked working in that area, with children and all that.

[She had] just turned 18 [when] she comes to me and says, I've met ... I've met a boy from Vilvoorde. She says, He wants to marry me. He came and introduced himself. He was an ordinary boy. He wore trendy clothes like all the other young guys. But I noticed he was possessive with her, too possessive. He was always behind her, with her. And afterwards I said to her, Oh listen Nora, oh listen to me. I don't want you to get married. You are too young. And she says to me, Oh, you won't hear about him anymore anyway. He has gone away.

I thought he'd gone somewhere to work. I didn't even know about Syria.

One Sunday, yes, on Sunday, I get up. [Nora] normally helps me out on Sundays and I don't see her come down from her bedroom [so] I go upstairs and I look and her bed is empty. I phone her and she says, Don't worry. She says, I'm just at the house of this young man's parents. Tarek's parents: the father's going to bring me back. Listen, I don't have any more credit or free texts. I won't be able to phone you again, but don't worry, I'm coming back tonight. I told her, Don't come back too late, I don't like it.

And [then] my son, the youngest, he also goes to Vivorrde, he gers back. My son is a pretty big guy. At the time he was 16 and a half. He was tall, 5 foot 9, but he weighed nearly 16 stone. And he comes back, and he never cries, he never shows his feelings. He comes in and starts pacing like he's been put in a cage. A wolf, erh, a lion in a cage. He starts pacing like that and he looks worried. He says, How am I going to tell you? I said, What's got into you? She's gone. She's gone. I said, but who's gone? Has someone had an accident? A friend? He said, No, no. She's gone. She's gone. But who? I kept asking. He says to me. Nora has gone to Syria. I said: You're mad. Gone to Syria? Why?

I really lived in another world.

She wanted to do something with her life. I, her mother, I'll regret it until I die, I didn't notice that little giveaway. I didn't see what she was missing.

They saw that weakness in her.

I found out she was often in Vilvoorde surrounded by [people] who manipulated her.

It took me 18 years to bring her up. And in a few months, they completely changed her. Completely.

Zarlasht Halamzai

[The history of Jihad is] both a very recent history and it can draw on a very old history. You now say Islam and the West, but basically it's the same thing as Islam and Christendom geographically, and that's a battle of over 1,300 years and there's so much rhetoric on both sides. And for about a 1,000 years of that time, the Muslims would have see themselves in the ascendant. It's really the last couple of hundred years that that's absolutely not been the case.

Moazzam Begg

Al Qaeda didn't exist in Iraq before the [2003] invasion. [The founder of Al Qaeda in Iraq] Abu-Musab al-Zarqawi moved from Afghanistan [to Iraq to] set it up. He wasn't part of Al Qaeda, but to get more credibility, he took on the name.

Shiraz Maher

Post the [Iraq] war people going to, you know, beach parties in Beirut, drinking whiskey, who [would ordinarily have] no truck with Al Qaeda, when they [saw] a US serviceman get blown [up] in Iraq [their response would be]: so don't be here. [This was] a very pervasive opinion. So Al Qaeda [was] relying on that goodwill to operate within Iraq.

[But] Zarqawi start[ed] to fuel the sectarian war with the Shia. [He became] really indiscriminate in the use of *takfir*, which is to excommunicate other Muslims [and thus justify their murder]. He started blowing up, you know, marketplaces and killing loads of Muslims, which meant, you know [that] Mr. Whiskey-swilling Beirut cosmopolitan young Muslim guy [said], whoa, fuck, it's not just the Americans they're after [when] they get through [with them, it's me that's] gonna be hanging from the lampposts. So, public opinion started to dissipate.

[Bin Laden's deputy at Al Qaeda central] sent a letter to Zarqawi [saying] stop, you're pissing everyone off, we need to keep public opinion. But Zarqawi defied the Al Qaeda [leadership,] something which had never happened [before]. He [brought] in other Sunni Jihadi groups who are fighting the US and the coalition. He died in 2006 [but] in in October of that year [these Sunni Jihadi groups] said we are gonna establish the Islamic state of Iraq. By 2010 Abu Bakr al-Baghdadi, [had risen] as leader.

Charlie Winter (Senior Research Associate at Georgia State University Transcultural Conflict and Violence Initiative)

What we saw in the, in the run up to Islamic State's declaration of the caliphate er, on the twenty-ninth of June 2014 was a very concerted campaign to expand the knowledge of why Abu Bakr al-Baghdadi would be a viable candidate, so tracing him directly back to the prophet, um interestingly through, through a Shiite er, ancestry and of course Islamic State is very much opposed to Shiite Muslims.

General John Allen (retired Marine four-star General who served as Obama's Special Presidential Envoy to the Global Coalition to Counter ISIL until November 12, 2015)

Daesh I'll use the Arabic term for it often, usually, in fact, is a lineal descendant of Abu Musab al-Zarqawi, and Abu Bakr al-Baghdadi, who is the so-called Caliph today, was one of Zarqawi's deputies.

Moazzam Begg

After Zarqawi was killed, it became under a series of leaders, Islamic State of Iraq. And when it moved over back into Syria it became Islamic State of Iraq and Syria: ISIS. And then back into Iraq again: Islamic State.

Charlie Winter

[There was also] a concerted campaign to [absorb] other er, jihadist and extremist Islamist [groups]. [They took care to stress] the close relationship the leaders of Islamic state had with the upper echelon of Al-Qaeda, for example Bin Laden, even though bridges had been burnt with Al-Qaeda and irreparable damage [had] been done between the, the two groups.

Moazzam Begg

The leadership of ISIS, were born out of the prisons of Abu Ghraib, and Camp Bucca, and Jordanian prisons, and, erm, Egyptian torture centres. Seventeen of the leaders of ISIS today had been held in Camp Bucca and Abu Ghraib prisons. It is there where they met many former Baathists, and the Baathists recognise that our system is over.

So they became Islamists [and they] formulated process which would see them both together, jointly, taking power.

It's not just about [power] actually, it's a complicated game. Most of the, the story now is based on a fault line, a baseline, which is the Shia and the Sunni.

Zarlasht Halamzai

The split in Islam between Shia and Sunni started right after the death of the prophet in 632, and centered around the question of who should become the first caliph – his son-in-law, Ali, or his father-in-law Abu Bakr. So it's initially about power and succession, though over the centuries you've had many theological and legal divisions as well. The history of Shia and Sunni relations varies greatly between regions and time periods, from co-operation and intermingling to violent enmity. Of course, you have the greatest enmity where the divide continues to involve a struggle for power, such as in Iraq. In most parts of the world such a struggle doesn't exist simply due to numbers – between 85% and 90% of the world's Muslims are Sunni.

But remember, there are 1.6 billion Muslims in the world and among those 1.6 billion you have Sunnis who kill Shia, Sunnis who think Shias are heretics but see no reason to want violence done to them, Sunnis who are prejudiced against Shias and wouldn't want their kids to marry them, Sunnis who wish they were Shia because they have better poetry etc.

And you have families like mine.

My mum's Shia, my dad's Sunni, and they constantly debate about their religions because, you know, my dad makes fun of my mum for her – like, you know, Shias are very eccentric. And then my mum makes fun of the fact that my dad's, you know, like a bit of a – uncouth, you know, kind of, like his version of Islam is kind of austere and doesn't have these beautiful traditions – and it's always been fine. No-one's died!

I call myself a Su-shi. I mean I don't go to the mosque all the time, but I think a large part of my values and everything is informed by Islam. [And] my parents never made us pick. They never said – You have to be Shia – except my mum occasionally would be like – You're a Shia, right? Yeah. But never – you know, they never made us kind of choose. But it's – yeah, it's been fine.

Moazzam Begg

When the Americans left Iraq, they put, er, Nouri al- Maliki in power, and he was Shiite but also very sectarian ... So once they came into Iraq, it was very easy for ISIS to take the Sunni areas. Even the Sunnis who hate ISIS, had to make a choice between either them or the Shiites, who were taking vengeance for the crimes of Saddam in the past.

General Allen

Saddamist elements, ah, empowered, um, Daesh. One of their principal objectives, of course, was to unhorse the central government, ah, in Baghdad, and to restore them once again to their previous, ah, level of influence and prestige. You know, I – as I was, ah, recruiting the tribes in 2007, to help us fight Al-Qaeda and ah, I constantly came across these pockets of Saddamist elements and they couldn't have cared less about Iraqis writ large – they couldn't have cared less, ah, about a well-governed or a democratic, ah, Iraq. All they cared about was the restoration of, of their power as Sunnis, ah, over the entire, ah, over, over Iraq and, and, ah, the entire Iraqi population.

On screen: scenes from the Caliphate: black flags, armed men in lines waving them.

A new section of the Eid 2013 video. This time another man with his name:

al Hanifah al-Belgi ji from Belgium

talking to camera.

Al Hanifah Al-Belgi

First of all I want to say to all the Muslims, may Allah accept from us and you. We hope for you a good year. In my whole life I never felt like a Muslim as I do now. Living amongst the Muslims and under the shade of the Khilafah. All praise is due to Allah, we are living here wonderfully in great happiness. We actually can wish for nothing more. And all praise is due to Allah.

the song swells

The Shari'ah of our Lord is light, by it we rise over the stars.
By it we live without humiliation, a life of peace and security.
The Shari'ah of our Lord is light, by it we rise over the stars.
By it we live without humiliation, a life of peace and security.

EID GREETINGS FROM THE LAND OF KHILAFAH

fade down music and turn screen blank as all three mothers occupy the stage

Samira

[Nora] rings me and she says, Mum, I'm in Syria. I came here to join my husband, I married him in a Muslim ceremony.

Two weeks later she rang us to tell me that he was dead, that he'd died with the soldiers [in a fight with] with Bashar Al Assad's soldiers, that he died 15 days after he'd arrived, that she'd lost the man she loved. *(Sigh.)*

She says to me: so he's dead, he died, Shahid. [Martyred]. *(Pause.)*

All that, that is what happened in 2013. *(Pause.)* When he died and everything.

I said to her: Come back. *(Worried.)* I said to her: Come back, my child. Come back, your life is here, this is your country, Belgium is not over there, it's not our war. She didn't say anything, *(Sad pause.)* She was so cold. She wasn't crying, nothing, because actually, they're not allowed to cry. I wanted to say to her: my child, I don't care that there's a war, I don't care. You're my child, I can't live without you.

Yasmin

[My son] talked politics like the rest of us. The fact that, well there's the problem of Palestine which comes up a lot. But that's not a reason to go. I have never asked him why he went, but perhaps it's the fact that he's never felt at home here and that there are lots of young people who've gone there so he thinks: they need me. There's this Muslim solidarity which is ingrained over there. [And] the fact that they all see the Coalition as being totally against one country, against one religion I mean, so that's very important. I think that's what it is.

Samira

[Nora] left on 20th May 2013. She left [a letter] for me. So, Mum. She says: Mum, erh, erh, I watched you bend over backwards for us, to buy us everything that we wanted. And she said: Well, we were shown videos about the Syrians, the women who are raped, the children living in the streets without parents. She wrote all this down. She says: So our duty, we have been told our duty is to go and help these people, no one's helping these people or anything. So I'm going there. I want to be like a mother and a father to these orphans.

Yasmin

My husband, it's been 8 years since he died, and I think if he were here, perhaps he wouldn't have gone.

Geraldine

To begin with [my son went not to ISIS but to] Jabhat al-Nusra. Jabhat al-Nusra was there more to help Syrians, rather than to fight. Now it's changed, right. They both fight, but to begin with, Jabhat al-Nusra was all about helping the Syrians to get away from Bashar's bombs.

It's in fact the police who told me what he was doing. He was in fact keeping watch behind Jabhat al-Nusra to make sure Bashar didn't in fact come from behind and attack. So that was a job for young people. They were in fact guards to begin with I mean. Erh. *(She exhales.)* He was part of those who could help. That's what he always said to me: I'm here to help.

IS tried to take soldiers from Jabhat al-Nusra. I think it was at a moment when the US had started to intervene that IS recruited lots of soldiers.

I said to him: don't ever sign up to the kamikazes. He said to me: Mum, I'm not stupid. I know that when you're a Muslim you can't do that. And if I am to remain a true Muslim, I will never put my name on that list.

Shiraz Maher

If I were Syrian, would I be fighting that regime? Damn right I would. It is a tyrannical regime that brutalises people. For every crime ISIS has committed, Assad has committed a comparable crime. Industrialised rape? He did it first. Beheading people, torturing people? He did it first. So, you know, we can't even say ISIS has pioneered new territory in terms of brutality. He's done every crime that they have done.

Zarlasht Halaimzai

Out of everybody that's fighting in Syria, I probably hate the Assad regime the most. As part of our work, my team spent months documenting attacks, including chemical attacks, on schools and on children. It was one of the most horrific experiences of my life and it was Assad who was bombing indiscriminately.

Charlie Winter

One of the estimates that I've seen, ah, and obviously it's nigh on impossible to [be sure] is that about 90% of civilians in Syria who have been killed have been killed by Assad as opposed to the jihadist groups

There's a huge disparity between the people who are going [to Syria]. Even with foreign fighters, from let's just take from Britain um, you'll have people going because they are bored here they don't feel like they're doing anything with their life they don't feel empowered. Going to join Islamic State [is] a very extreme form of countercultural rebellion. You'll have people who really believe in the ideology or who really revel in, instances of Islamic say ultra-violence. I think it's important to recognize this variation.

Moazzam Begg

Er, sadly I think that a lot of the youth, who are a.) primarily not Arabic speakers, from the UK – mostly South Asian, b.) very young, c.) inexperienced, and, and ironically, really don't know very much about their faith. Um, so they're reacting to numerous things. [Part of the] pull factor is this: ISIS claims it is the re-establishment of the long foretold caliphate on the methodology of the prophet: the prophetic traditions about foretelling the, the end of time; the great battles that will take place in Damascus; Jesus himself returning as Muslims believe; and the wings of white angels descending on the minarets of Damascus, I mean it's very powerful terminology. And the fact that the Americans and the Western forces are attacking them. They cite this quotation of Imam Ali who was the fourth caliph who said if you want to know where the people of virtue are, look to the arrows of the enemies, and follow them.

The push factor is the media, laws, politicians, experiences, Twitter, Facebook, all telling you that you don't belong. That every single day there's one story or another, that's blown out of all proportion, that is talking negatively about you. It's not saying that this is a British thing, that the problem is a British one, it's saying it's a Muslim problem. And it doesn't matter if it's a French Muslim, or an Algerian Muslim, it's just a Muslim problem. So the more we're told that, the more people – especially the youth, I think, simply think, I've had enough.

Four young people also are on stage – two male, two female. They are six form school pupils from Tower Hamlets. They are called A (male) B (female) C (female) and D (male) because they are anonymous. They are talking together about the issues [possible interviewer present] sometimes they jump in and talk over each other. They are being interviewed about their views.

Male A

The general of America, right, he said that – Michael T. Flynn, that's what's his name, right – he said "We are at war against Muslims". So that would encourage Muslims – but it wouldn't encourage me – but it encourages some Muslims who are maybe less knowledgeable to join ISIS.

I think we are being picked on: like, for example erm the Daily Mail when erm in The Great British Bake Off when Nadia won, the Somali Muslim, they were saying that she won but then she came from Leeds and then they said that that, "Ah, that's where the three bombers came from." Like, what has that got to do with her winning the British er Bake Off? It's like they tried to build a bridge between terrorism and Muslims.

Male D

I think with the Charlie Hebdo, it's the same thing that keeps happening in the media. They keep thinking that ones who go and bomb people [are Muslims] ...

Female B *(Over talking.)*

They are – but they don't represent all of us.

Male D *(Over talking.)*

... they don't represent all the Muslims,

Female C

It's like ... they stereotype it, yeah.

Male D

They stereotype it. We – we – we live in the society and we don't have ideas of bombing places every day.

Female C

We're normal British citizens.

Male D

Just living a normal life.

Mohammed Akunjee (Solicitor who deals with terrorism or extreme Muslim related matters: solicitor to the three Bethnal green families.)

There are elements in the community that will look at what um what western forces [did] in Iraq. Um not just in terms of invading it and the effect on the civilian population but issues like Abu Ghraib prison where individuals were tortured, raped, maimed. And ISIS quite cleverly were dressing up their victims in orange suits as a nod and a wink to the Guantanamo situation but actually more importantly to the Abu Ghraib situation

Male A *(Whispers.)*

I didn't know.

Female B *(Whispers.)*

You didn't know?

Male D *(Whispers.)*

You didn't know?

Male A

I didn't know that they were dressed in orange.

Female B

For that specific reason.

Mohammed Akunjee

So um, effectively what they're saying is you treat our people with no regard to international law and nothing happens to the perpetrators so we will treat yours in the same way. It's the law of Moses which is an eye for an eye and a tooth for a tooth.

Those four girls [who went from Bethnal Green] and some others had basically created a clique and they were, you know they were influencing each other. And the first girl certainly was a great influence. She ... she ... she had a very difficult family situation really. Um, her mother had died um some months before. Her father very quickly remarried. Um, you know she became aware that her, her father's wife was pregnant. She'd completely disconnected from her family unit. Her identity was effectively gone um, and ... and she'd looked outside of the family unit for I guess a sense of identity. And she saw more of family in the ... in the um propaganda of ISIS which talks about a brotherhood of men and what have you ... than she did at home. And she, certainly spouted that loud and clear. Not on the internet but amongst her friendship circle.

Reverend Doctor Paul Fitzpatrick (Chaplain and Researcher into radicalisation and grooming at Cardiff Metropolitan University)

Anybody can be groomed: if you're at a weak point in your life, you happen to meet a bad patch; if you're a young girl in the bedroom in Glasgow, you know, you're fourteen or fifteen years old and you're feeling lonely you don't like the repression at home, you love the fact that your friends can go out dancing, drinking, or mobile phones or whatever. Or [you're] the young lad that's been bullied or punched half his life. Sometimes you're somebody who's got none of that, you know, a recent convert who's – who's just revelling in the fact that he's finally found himself, in this great God that – that – that envelopes him and holds him into a community where he has status and meaning and function.

If I wanted to recruit somebody, what I would do – and I've seen this done, and it's very effective – I'd print a poster, a flyer; I'd put a mobile number on it, um and I'd make it ambiguous, but I would promise meals or help – "Are you having a bad time in your life? Do you need some support? Come and meet the brothers at this number." Something simple but something with a big visual image. Then you don't stick it on top of the notice board. What you do is you – you – you, you lift all the other bits of paper on the notice board and you put, underneath them, this – this X or Y. erm, and then – then you put the other notice things back on the board so that it's at least partially if not fully covered. And what happens is, then you're hiding your message from people that are scanning the boards who should go by, but the people who find that X and Y are the people who are looking for something.

Helen Ball (Deputy Assistant Commissioner within the Metropolitan Police and Senior National Co-ordinator Counter Terrorism Policing)

In the early days [of the Syrian conflict] we would be looking at this phenomenon, thinking about, you know, what are the motivations for people going, um, but absolutely understood that many people are going simply for humanitarian motives.

Those people by and large they've all stopped [going to Syria] because they've seen what's happening and they know how dangerous it is and that they also actually don't want to be part of that environment.

What interests me is that some people appear to be able to reconcile, um, joining an organisation which they must [now] know is, is murdering and torturing people.

They must know that but yet they still go and join it and I don't understand how they manage to reconcile that. [There are] people with that huge sense of grievance. Um, I acknowledge that, that they genuinely have that, that sense of grievance and anger, um, but not compounding it by going and joining an organisation that's doing the very same thing and worse.

Paul Fitzpatrick

You know how grooming works? "I love you I love you I love you come to me." And at a given point *(sound of a slap)* either violence or control, power, money, something – but there's a slap. At the end there is violence. "Oh! It must be my fault! He's so lovely, he's so wonderful." "Come to me come to me come to me." And gradually this grooming process changes the way you think.

Exactly the same thing's happening in those [ISIS] videos, [you've got] wonderful pictures, pictures of the young men from Cardiff, [for example] who are under the erm the date trees and they're in a circle, they've all got their Kalashnikovs, they're all down on one knee, they're all like – they're talking directly to camera – they are presentable, they are beautiful. But at the end of these videos, there's always violence, you know? And so you get this – "You're with us you're with us come and join us – be part of the Islam which is servitude, which is submission to this greater cause, you know, and be part of this army because we are destroying our enemies." They're – they're two themes of power. And I know they're – they're – they're opposed and because you're very sophisticated and normal, happy human being[s], you – you recognise that – the, the, the difference between them. Vulnerable people often do not.

Charlie Winter

We all hear about the beheadings and things like that but er far and away the most prominent element of its propaganda is the utopian image it has for itself.

Someone says that you can be a founding member of a new utopian state which is implementing God's will on Earth and is the only place that you can truly be engaged with your religion and also fight on behalf of your co-religionists the world over er and you'll have er a great bunch of friends and you'll also have wives and you'll also have um, economic sustenance and you'll be living in this beautiful er historic and theologically important land in Syria. I mean that's quite a powerful argument um. Of course it doesn't resonate with everyone but to some people it will.

On screen: some of these idyllic images alternating with the occasional sinister one.

[When you look at ISIS propaganda you don't only see violence] You see schools operating healthcare, er distribution of benefits, distribution of er, butchered meats to celebrate Eid, roads being cleaned etc. The amount of really bizarre photos I see showing hosepipe factories and stone masonry factories and er, honey being harvested um zoos, loads of zoos er particularly in the last month for some reason. It's selling itself as a comprehensive er alternative to societies in which we live in now, come and join us to be a part of this. I think that's a very powerful thing.

Shiraz Maher

It's like a communist utopia. Everyone toils for the state. Everyone produces labour that [serves] the state and that's what makes, you know, their lives so meaningful.

So, when people ask about the women who go off to join ISIS, you have to understand it from their perspective. They are contributing to something that's bigger than themselves, that has meaning, purpose and it's for the greater good of Islam, for the creator of everything.

Paul Fitzpatrick

I think the only common factor that I've come across is that when people join a radicalised group, it's because there's something empty in them. I don't mean a big empty. That's easier to identify and it's quite easy in place to deal with that. I think that the majority that I've worked with that have been radicalised the need is much more subdued. It's a cognitive opening, a searching, a slight need for identity, for discovering themselves. People like Ranulph Fiennes go up mountains and go into the wilds – they find their identity in doing that. Everyone that I've known who – who has brushed some form of radical group has had a distinct but subtle need, emptiness, longing. A – a requirement to move on, [a vulnerability]. I use vulnerability but not in the sense that the government would use it, that this is someone you can hurt, because – that's not how I mean it – I mean someone who has positively opened themselves to look at another way of being. Now, with all good learning that happens you take risk when you, you learn. But with people that have been radicalized, they've taken risk with their identity, their story, who they are, their structure, their society.

Shiraz Maher

When you're in everything makes sense. Even when you get it wrong, it doesn't matter because, you know, it comes from God, right. So, you go and you win and God will reward in you. [And if] it all fails and blows up in your face. God is testing you. Either way the same solution: you redouble your efforts, you get closer to God. So, there's no way you can lose cos you're serving God.

I've interviewed a hundred ISIS members of which a good, vast chunk are Brits and when I talk to them it's like talking to myself 10, 15 years ago. One of them I really felt bonded. I was like, you are just like me, and he made me actually realise, when I was talking to him [that] I'm lucky that 9/11 was my thing. If I was 20 now, would I have joined ISIS? Bloody good chance. I say that to Michael Justice [the Justice Secretary]. [I say] I'm sitting here now talking to you having left Hisb ut-Tahrir which, you think is not as serious as ISIS but you have to understand these guys are operating on exactly the same wavelength. It's exactly the same stuff.

The youth today feel at loggerheads with society. Then there's the broader issue: what is my role in society? That applies to, you know, white working classes who are saying we've been disenfranchised, we have no role anymore, um, right down to the Muslim guys saying, this society's got nothing for me, and there is a general breakdown of sort of liberal society where individuals don't know what their purpose is.

Male D

David Cameron, you know. Recently he said that British Muslim women have to, erm, learn English or, erm, face, erm, deportation. He's really alienating and just focusing on one ethnic minority and one particular group.

Female C

Why is it just Muslim women? Why can't it be all? And why women? Why can't it be everyone?

Male A

Someone says the word 'terrorist', it's almost like automatically in your head the word 'Muslim' comes before it, because the media, esp – newspapers and the TV, usually [use] the tag of 'Muslim terrorist' or erm 'Muslim man does this', but when it comes to other people, there isn't that tag. It's – yeah – it'll be, like, "Oh, a *man* just does this," or erm "A rapist does this".

Female C

Sometimes I wear, wear skirts; sometimes I wear jeans. Sometimes when I'm wearing skirts I feel worried that people think, Oh, that girl was forced into wearing that. And that kind of makes me think about my actions and – makes me think, Oh, actually maybe I shouldn't [or], maybe I should just [to] prove to people that I *can* do this. I think that's happened to a lot of young people nowadays, cos they feel like they have to act in a certain way to show people that I'm not an extremist. Like [after], all these young people, especially the girls that went from Tower Hamlets, I feel as if now because it's hit so close to me, I feel as if I have to just prove [I'm not an extremist].

Female B

Sometimes when I go on the train I have people literally, just stare at me for a very long time and that kind of paranoia is, what is there to stare at? Because there's other people in the carriage and you are only staring at me and that makes me think, is it 'cos of the way I'm dressing or like, is it because I'm wearing like a hijab or something.

Male A

There are some words in, in public, like say, 'explode' or 'explosion' – I could be on the tube and I could be talking to somebody next to me about a firework show and be like, "A firework went up and it exploded" but I would be really cautious of who heard it. Or I would just completely avoid the subject of mentioning anything like that, because people automatically they'll turn and they'll look, "Oh, have you got a bag on you, are your pockets a little bit bulging?" or something like that.

Female C

Yeah.

Male D

I feel like the same. Like like sometimes if I just have to like put my bag down to like fix my jacket and suddenly I just have all these faces like turning at me and I feel like kind of like "I'm not doing anything, I'm just putting my bag down to fix my jacket!" and I think, like, there's a paranoia around it.

fade up sound that is the first reports of the attacks in Paris – soft at first

Abu Bakr al-Baghdadi (Reading from, _The Management of Savagery_ a 2004 strategy document for Al Qaeda and other jihadists)

The overwhelming military power [of the west] has no value without the cohesion of society. Motivate crowds, particularly the youth, to fly to the regions which we manage. Diversify the strikes against the Crusader-Zionist enemy in every place in the Islamic world, and even outside it, and thus drain it ... Work to expose the weakness of America's [and its allies'] power by pushing it to abandon the war by proxy until it fights directly.

the sounds are getting louder

General Allen

I was asked by the President of the United States in August of 2014 to serve as his Special Presidential Envoy to the Global Coalition to Counter ISIL, a job, ah, that I held until November 12, 2015. A conversation [in the White House] on my last day of November 12th was that we need to be very attentive, ah, of the globalising threat of ISIL. And then on the 13th [my] phone vibrated briefly, and there was a BBC news alert, talking about shooting occurring in Paris. I've experienced many times over the years in various positions that I've had, the reporting that a shooting is occurring and there are some number of casualties, and then you just know that it's going to get bigger and it's going to get worse and, ah, I watched the reporting unfold over the next 24-48 hours, and it was quite, quite gruesome ...

More audio snatches of what happened in 2015 in Paris along with images from the Bataclan and other sites of attacks, both during the attack and in the aftermath.

Intercut these with stills of ISIS fighters, or orange clad people on the way to being executed, and also of Syrian civilians after attacks from Assad or others. In short, an impressionist portrayal of the violence that erupts not only in Syria but also in Paris.

Male D

When I first [heard] about the attacks in Paris obviously I felt shocked and my heart went out to the victims, but then after that I feel like being a Muslim myself I feel double the fear of what others would feel. Because now I know, from this attack, my Muslim identity is going to be villainised more ... I feel like people look at me differently.

You, you see that, erm, Donald Trump, and that, making these statements an you know, I knew that was going to come.

Female B

I think that because it happened in Paris, it's much more, erm, emphasised. It's it's a city that everybody knows, it's a city that, you know, loads of people go to. Whereas [when bombs go off in] places like Iraq ... Much emphasis isn't put on it.

Male D

I think [the day before Paris] something happened in Lebanon, as well, a bomb. People died, Not ... Obviously not 132, but about [40] people or so died and ... they didn't portray it in an equal way.

Female C

It should be given as much coverage as an attack in Paris. It's not fair.

Female B

[And recently] there were suicide bombings in Istanbul, There was really like huge commotion over what happened in Paris and I was just wondering how come the same treatment, or same reactions can't happen for Istanbul? Is it because maybe it's a Muslim city, or is it because Paris is closer to us?

Female C

I, in France, after the attacks, basically a lot of countries, were projecting like the French flag on their, erm, what was it called? Landmarks.

Male A

Monuments.

Female C

Monuments. But you know, there's wars other places. Why don't you look at them, as well? Why is it just that the western country when it's under attack people look at it?

General Allen

[Daesh] is going to take this war to us in as many ways as possible. Um, at the heart of [its] doctrine [is that] it must be in relentless war with all of us, ah, and it must be a war that expands its surface area and expands the numbers of people that it subjugates.

Charlie Winter

Islamic State is the provider of ah, a modicum of stability in a war zone, and ah, an organisation that encourages enterprise among the local population – I mean, it is the, ah, the least worst option for a great many people in Syria and Iraq, and, and it's trying to cultivate this image of being the Sunni protector. I think that that's as important as this war against the West – probably actually more important.

General Allen

Our intention is to cut off the lines of movement to and out of Raqqa, but we don't intend to enter and clear it. I'm a Marine, and it was Marines who cleared Fallujah – I spent 13 months in Fallujah, so I will tell you that that was horrific fighting. Um, our intention is ultimately to, ah, pressure Daesh in multiple ways, to confine it in Raqqa [until it] becomes less relevant as the capital. The intent then is for us to continue to empower Syrian Arabs, Kurds, Iraqi Kurds and Iraqi Arabs to be the defeat mechanism of Daesh.

Charlie Winter

Containing [Islamic State] in Syria and letting them rot. Well, I mean, sure, it could work, but I just don't think that it's at all feasible. The Kurds will only go as far as, ah, as, as they're comfortable going; um, the Shiite militias – I mean, they will also only go as far as they feel comfortable going, unless they have an expansionist tendency, which is, which is even more troubling than, ah, than, than not going in in the first place. [Pushing Islamic State out of] Iraq and Syria, [is] much easier said than done, um, and it doesn't deal with the fact that this is an insurgency rather than just this terrorist group, and it's an insurgency that has spent a lot of time trying to entrench itself with the local population, and it's learnt from past mistakes. Ah, yes, it's very brutal. Yes, it is, ah, kind of notorious in its meting out of executions, etc, but at the same time it is trying to keep the population on side.

Shiraz Maher

ISIS is run well because it has guys who have done this. It's got a brilliant intelligence service because, again, lots of former Mukhabarat, the secret service of the, ah, of the [Iraqi] state, is involved with them. [And] you know, if we presented ourselves at the border now, we could join ISIS pretty easily, all of us. You just have to say, you're comrades. ISIS take anyone in, so they have a large army but also they took in large numbers of Bosnians and Chechens who have really good insurgent experience. The most valuable asset any military has is troops with combat experience and all these guys have fought the Russians, have fought in Bosnia, they know what they're doing. Combine them with the Baathists, it's a proper military.

Let's be very generous here, [there were] 1,000 people in Al Qaeda in 2001 when they attacked the United States: you're looking at 30 times the size right now in a far more permissive environment, in a far more entrenched space with really sophisticated weaponry. I mean, the Taliban didn't have much between them. You know, ISIS, they've got stuff.

Charlie Winter

In the future, if they do eventually get pushed out of Iraq and Syria, then Libya will be a fall-back option, simply because it is characterised by immense political disarray. But the common denominator here, is that Islamic State support for violent extremist groups is, is a symptom of deeply entrenched political disarray and discontent. ISIS worsens the cycle of violence, but it is not purely a cause of, of, ah, of this [violence].

Shiraz Maher

I don't believe ISIS will be in military decline for quite some time. It has an army that's roughly half the size of the British Army. And there isn't a power in the world today that has the ability to remove it. Militarily none of the regional powers can and politically the Western powers can't commit to it. We don't have the finances and we don't have the public support and, if you were going to, you'd have to prepare the public for probably about a 20-year occupation of both Syria and Iraq and for tens of thousands of casualties as opposed to 300 British casualties in the last war. So it's not gonna happen. Even if it were to happen, even if the state broke up: you are looking at you know, maybe 20,000/30,000 fanatical devotees around the world. I don't really call them terrorist group, they're much more than that. This is a millenarian state project, that is armed to the teeth and it goes, I suppose, by definition because a millenarian, they go down by dying and taking everyone down with them.

General Allen

The theory behind a Caliphate is that the Caliph, ah, has, has been both uniquely uniquely selected ... to lead meaning both his spiritual and his, ah, academic, ah, and his leadership qualities were such that he was the, um, the, ah, choice of the central Shura. He's a pretty important figure for the practical leadership on a day-to-day basis, but he's an extraordinarily important figure for the spiritual leadership and ... the Caliphate. I think taking out Abu Bakr al-Baghdadi could have, ah, quite a, quite a substantial, um, [effect]. And I'll just simply say that we're thinking now about the day we get him. So that we don't all wake up one morning and a Hellfire missile had effect, and now we all stand around looking at our feet, we're thinking right now about what comes next, and typically what comes next is kill the number two man, the second we find him, or go after what we think is the senior leadership pool. In effect we are going after the entire central nervous system.

Charlie Winter

The cult of personality around Baghdadi is nowhere near as robust or resilient as the cult of statehood around the Islamic State Caliphate. The symbolic value of it being declared is, is more important than who exactly has declared it. And I think it's, it's possibly short-sighted to think, ah, that Baghdadi being killed or, or kind of senior leadership being killed would cause the group to evaporate. I mean, it's more an idea than a true organisation. Yes you can really harm the group tactically, but strategically, in the long run, it's going to carry on existing as an idea. The only way it can be beaten as an idea is by a better alternative.

I would totally be pro-intervention over Syria, ah, if I thought that there was a real strategy behind it [and a] real intention to, to understand that Assad is, ah, Islamic State's greatest recruiting sergeant and that with Assad in power, ah, then there is no solution to what we are seeing now emanating from Syria and Iraq. But for as long as there is a reluctance to implement meaningful reform, this, this situation will continue. And I just think that the rhetoric coming out of Westminster and the, ah, the rest of the capitals across the world is that, is that Islamic State can be beaten just by, um, by technical prowess and by, ah, resolve. It deeply, deeply troubles me.

Paul Fitzpatrick

All we seem to do in the West and with Russia now is just go and bomb even more, and I just don't see that as an answer and I think in a sense, that encourages people to go and fight, you know? Iraq was the same, Afghanistan was the same. Again I will support ... I wear a poppy, I support our service people to nth degree but I do not see any reason why we are fighting those wars. I really don't.

Charlie Winter

It's a fallacy to think that air strikes will do anything, ah, to harm Islamic State's longevity. Um, anyone who's anyone in the group is not going to be sitting in a building, ah, in Raqqa. Um, yes, Emwazi [Jihadi John] was killed there, but he, he was just a figurehead – he wasn't someone who was in the upper echelons of the group, and to think that through kind of decapitation and air strikes we can, we can remove the threat that it poses, um, that's just wrong.

Paul Fitzpatrick

The problem is even if we were to be military successful – if we sent all the troops in, what do we get when it's all over? Again? Maybe we destroy ISIS, but then Al-Qaeda becomes a fire again.

Charlie Winter

Terrorism in this day and age, ah, and this will be a controversial thing to say, is, ah, as necessary an evil as car crashes and plane crashes – it's going to happen and we need to deal with it, but we need to deal with it in a way that is rational and doesn't, ah, fall into the, the strategy of the people who are planning these attacks. And what they are craving above and beyond anything else is to provoke, to polarise and to escalate, We need to understand that things that appear counterintuitive to us, like escalation, are actually desirable to [them].

fade up the Eid music

Abu Bakr al-Baghdadi May 14, 2015

And if the Crusaders today claim to ... to confine themselves to targeting the armed amongst [the Muslim public], then soon you will see them targeting every Muslim ... And if the Crusaders today have begun to harass the Muslims who ... live in the lands of the cross by monitoring them, arresting them, and questioning them, then soon they will begin to displace them and ... either [kill them], imprison [them] or [make them] homeless.

Zarlasht Halamzai

I've worked on the border of Syria for 18 months, and one of – like the best way to find out what was happening across the border was go through Twitter, and you look at Nusra fighters, you look at ISIS fighters, because they're the ones who are fighting, so you're looking at what's happening through their Twitter accounts. But when we, when we had our conversation [about doing this interview] I went and looked for the blogs that I used to read, and some of them had been taken down. I got so paranoid, and I started thinking about what I would say if there was – you know, if I was arrested – like why am I looking at this stuff?

Female C

I wouldn't erm like personally like google like ISIS. The only times where I like – you know – read about it or thing is when it's in the news or like when it's on erm like newspaper

– I wouldn't like personally like – gone about like searching it or anything.

Male D

because you don't know erm – like the government, they might think that you're ...

Male A

Might track you.

Female C

They might like eh survey you and think that you're part of the people who are becoming radicalised. So it's like that kind of fear on you.

Male A

If I'm being truly honest, I have to think twice about everything I say in this conversation even though my name's not going to be said.

Female C

I kind of agree erm like, yesterday I went to do some research on ISIS, like in preparation for this! *(Laughs.)*

Male D

Yeah, me too!

Female C

I was actually really scared to research it.

Male A

Yeah, I left the tab open and I got a bit scared! *(Laugh.)* So quickly X'd it.

Male D

We were still like fearful like the government *(laughs)* were watching over us and stuff!

Mohammed Akunjee

Since 2000 there's been a number of changes in the law particularly the Terrorism Act 2000 and 2006 [which] have extended or created offences which simply didn't exist before in the UK, unless you go back to sort of Oliver Cromwell's time where we have ideas of thought crime or it being illegal to um own books or material that to a a prosecutor's mind would be relevant to terrorists or terrorism. And terrorists and terrorism have a very much wider sort of definition [nowadays]. Um and it encompasses things like having information likely to be of use to terrorists. Um that can include theological books. It can include um treatises on a religious discourse or ... or I ... legal discourse. It never ever says that it's specifically for the Muslim faith, that would be discriminatory in itself. Um but the law provides enough discretion and the practice of it shows that it is almost exclusively towards the Muslim community.

Human beings can deal with being told you can't say something. What they can't deal with very well, and rightly so, is where they feel that it's un ... there's a lack of justice or lack of fair play. Britain has always prided itself on its sense of fair play and balance. And that's its core values, core principles. And I think we've lost our way.

David Cameron (Prime Minister's speech at Ninestiles school in Birmingham on July 10th 2015)

We are all British. We respect democracy and the rule of law. We believe in freedom of speech, freedom of the press, freedom of worship, equal rights regardless of race, sex, sexuality or faith.

Female B

[Those values] are shared all around the world. Why do we have to put a label on it that this is British. It's human rights.

Female C

While they're trying to enforce something that's supposed to make us more united, it's making us feel more segregated. The idea of British values is kind of playing on,

Oh, okay, I'm [don't] feel a part of these British values, I've got – I've got erm Muslim values as well, or I've got Bengali or Somalian values as well. Maybe I should go join Muslim values in a different country.

Male D

I think subliminally [talk of British values] is having problems with the younger people. Me, when I'm doing erm – what are they called – questionnaires and the nationality part comes up, I don't know if I should tick the Bengali box or the British Bengali box or the British box. I don't know what I am because, am I British, so am I like denying my Bengali background? Or if I'm British Bengali, would the British not accept me because I'm saying "I'm half half". Like, is there such a thing as dual nationality?

Moazzam Begg

David Cameron [made that speech] ironically in the school, erm that my son goes to – that son was born while I was in Guantanamo, while I was being interrogated by British intelligence agents – he came to that school and he gave a talk about extremism. And he gave points about what he said extremism is. And one of them is a refusal to accept democracy. Another is to be intolerant of other people's beliefs. Another he said was the rejection of the rule of law.

How many people in this country since the beginning of the war on terror either directly or indirectly have been renditioned, have been falsely imprisoned, have been tortured, with British complicity? Where's the rule of law there?

Prevent [the government's programme to stop extremism and radicalisation], prior to this was a voluntary thing. If you felt someone was radicalised you could contact Prevent officers and get them into a Channel programme [which is individually tailored to help them]. Now as a result of the Counter Terrorism and Security Act 2015, Prevent is law. If you're a professor at university or a lecturer or a doctor or a nurse, if you see somebody who you think is becoming radicalised, then you're obliged to report it to the Prevent officers, i.e. the police.

Charles Farr (former Director General of the Office of Security and Counterterrorism and current Chair of the Joint Intelligence Committee which sits in the Cabinet Office)

It's not Police-lead. I mean ... a very wide range of statutory organisations very far from policing are themselves involved in Prevent uh, in their own way, not according to instructions issued to them by local Policing. Of course, the Police have to be involved because many Prevent Programmes are of ... are of relevance to the Police and Police information needs to be used to inform Prevent Programmes because the Police will have arrested people who, uh, um, whose ... whose history is relevant to the way we do Prevent. So we need to understand and get information about and from the Police to ensure that Prevent is doing what it should do which is to stop the radicalisation of the people in this country.

Prevent is fundamentally about protecting those people. If they go to Syria and Iraq, they will almost certainly be killed, and before they're killed, they will be treated in a way that no one would wish on anyone and it seems to me that is what Prevent is doing, is trying to stop, and I have yet to hear what the alternative is. Does the State leave people to get groomed by organisations online or offline and encouraged to go to Syria? Does the State stand back and say, "That is their responsibility, it is up to them whether they wish to go and get themselves killed?"

Really? I don't think, you know, in my experience, that's the view of most Muslim communities.

Mohammed Akunjee

We are supposed to be a pluralist society which allows freedom of thought and expression. The legitimacy of those ideas are tested by our reaction to people who speak things that we don't agree with and maybe are repugnant. I think we're in a very dangerous time when we're talking about the censorship of ... of ... of non normative ideas.

One of the seven factors [in the Prevent strategy] is that you know men start, or boys start growing beards and women start wearing hijabs. The problem with that is that girls start wearing hijabs just out of religious conservatism at the age of puberty.

It ... it ... it's simply not a factor that helps anyone understand whether someone's been radicalised or not.

Shiraz Maher

The [current] Prevent strategy is bolder, it's smarter, it's wiser in some aspects [than the] Labour one [but] what they've given with one hand they've taken away with the other. The Terrorism Act was drafted deliberately vaguely because it needs to be malleable to events. And I think Prevent operates in the same way but the point is that's not a model that society should operate on. They are sort of getting to a result of pre-crime, getting into thought policing.

DAC Ball

You know, one of the reasons why people have concerns about Prevent is because they only see ... visibly see police operating that area, so they assume it's criminalising and it isn't.

It's not [police led]. [Teachers] can simply draw support from the Department for Education, for example, um, or within their own school, um, to deal with whatever it is they're seeing. Um, there's no reason to bring it to police unless they feel that they, ah, they need to.

It's not just about extreme ideas, it's about violence, um, aggression, anger, um, and it can be that somebody's being abused by being radicalised in that way by somebody else. So, I think there are enough similarities for us to work within safeguarding procedures.

Tufyal Choudhury (Durham university law lecturer and researcher into the impact of counter-terrorism measures on Muslim communities in the UK)

It is different from other forms of safeguarding because you're trying to identify children that you think you're safeguarding society from. You're saying this person is a risk, not that they're themselves at risk. That's a different, erm, call. The other thing is the involvement of counter-terrorism and policing in all of this, and security services.

So if you're exploring identity, becoming more religious, erm, all of those things become pathologised, as indicators of risk. When for anybody else, those would just be an indicator of being a teenager *(laughing)*. And, you know, if you're a, if you're a teacher, or a youth worker, or a college, erm, lecturer, you think, well should I not therefore refer this, just in case this might be somebody who's, you know, who later turns out to, you know, become a terrorist.

DAC Helen Ball

They have a statutory duty to prevent people getting involved in extremism. They need to exercise their responsibilities under that duty and if the default position is that they or somebody else rings up the police and we go and deal with that issue, that just brings it all into the criminal space where it needn't be. So, the art of this is going to be responsible institutions delivering public services, recognising their responsibilities.

Tufyal Choudhury

My concern is that teachers are going to be risk averse. So they get their training, and they're gonna be told what are indicators. And we're already seeing a few reports of this, of examples of, erm, school, you know, of pupils being asked to speak to the local Channel, or Prevent coordinator, because of something they'd said in the classroom. And I think, if you're the teacher, would you want to take that risk of missing somebody?

Shiraz Maher

I have a statutory obligation, if I think [my students are] being radicalised, to report them. So, I threatened to report them all regularly just to cover my back. I mean, that's how ridiculous it is. So, I'm just gonna report all of you and then, then it's not in my hands anymore. I've covered myself. *(Chuckles.)* Right?

fade up an echo from the Management of Savagery

Work to expose the weakness of America's [and its allies']
power by pushing it to abandon the war by proxy until it
fights directly.

Charlie Winter

I [do] think that [the November events in Paris] certainly is a game-changer in terms of how we would understand Islamic State's global ambitions. But I still don't think that it means that Islamic State represents an existential threat to us. It's a symptom of a great many different problems the world over. And yes, Paris was a very frightening event and, and showed that Islamic State was willing, as did the Russian airliner, was willing to embark upon, ah, large scale attacks against us in the West in the pursuit of its, its jihadist project. But it's how we respond that poses the greatest threat. [The attacks] are geared towards causing hasty reactions, ill-thought-out reactions, security-led reactions that, that go on to assist the cause of, ah, terrorist recruitment and polarisation. So it doesn't need to be an existential threat unless we let it be. I think that the reaction post Paris, the rise of the Far Right, the rising anti-Muslim sentiment in Europe is because people are falling into the trap that terrorists are setting for us. I think the existential threat lies in how we respond to it, rather than the kind of things that it can do to us.

Male D

One individual coming over and bombing and killing a few people is not a bigger threat than a whole nation yeah going and taking over whole country. I think the terrorism also gets exaggerated. And we always report the – kind of the Muslim erm terrorism but there's other forms of terrorist as well who probably oppose the government or who disagree with the government and al – also tried certain things that are radical we don't really hear much about them in the media.

Male A

Er I was with my mates at Oxford Circus and There was a group of female French women calling like, erm, three or four Bengali or Asian boys ISIS, go back to your country and basically it was havoc, there was going to be an actual fight. It was really intense. they were saying, you're ISIS, go, go get passport ... Don't bomb me, ... But they couldn't speak English properly and we kind of had to calm the situation down or it was going to be like a full-blown fight. And it was quite ironic cause they were French and they were say, go back to your own country when the other boys were clearly from Britain, as well. It was really weird for me. It was quite scary, as well.

Male D

The media ain't really saying enough about, let's say, erm the Ku Klux Klan, or the EDL [or other organisations that threaten us].

[Why is that?]

I think – I think that's a question that the people who are watching this play should – should ... ask themselves.

[What I'd like to say to you is that] we are exactly the same as you, that's what I think Every fear that you feel whenever you see these attacks or stuff, we feel it, as well. It's not as if we don't.

fade up the Eid music and then fade it down

The stage is empty now, saved for the three Belgian mothers.

Samira

[Nora] never says which group they're in. They don't speak freely. You get the impression there's always someone with them. Me, what I noticed is that that ... she spoke like a robot And when you ask her questions, they shut down And they won't say another word. [She] wears a niqab. You can't see her face, you only see her eyes, that's all. You only see her eyes.

My daughter, I'm going to tell you something. I saw her once on the Internet ... She's nothing like the beautiful girl who was here. It gives you a shock. She's a young girl who has aged. She's 20 but you would easily give her ... frankly, my age. Who's so thin ... very, very, very thin.

Yasmin

I still try to make contact with [Karim]. It's not easy because he doesn't agree with the way I live here. The fact that I'm not out there with him. I said to him: I'll come and see you.

I'm happy to risk my life to go and see him, to be able to have him in my arms again, but he doesn't want to see me if it's just for a few hours, a few days. He told me the pain would be too much for him.

Samira

The house is dead. She was someone, [energetic] you could hear her, she was loud, she had my personality. She was someone, we loved to argue; we went out together, we shared things. And just going down the stairs, you would hear bambambambam.

She would shout, she had a strong personality. It was, you could hear her, it was full of life.

It's very hard but every time I speak about her she lives. She is living.

I laugh, I smile and everything, but it's not the same smile as before. It's like there's, I don't know, something inside of me that's going out, a flame … a flame which is dimming a little more every day. Every time I sleep, as my children say, I eat Nora, I sleep with Nora, I live Nora, I speak about Nora. I can't … I can't live without her …

Yasmin

When [Karim's] talking to me, I hear: brother, brother. He talks about boys who are over there, men, there are … I say to him: who are you talking to? To my brother. I say: Oh, right. I didn't know I had children over there. He says: no, it's my brother.

[He was wounded]. He phoned me. He said … it's not too serious. And a few days later, he was wounded again. The first time he was wounded, it was one of Bashar's helicopters, from Bashar's side who were dropping explosives and there were some shard … shards. And after they'd been bombed, they were in a house and there were several people with him who died. And he was wounded. *(Pause.)* I … And since then I've been very scared.

The last time I was able to speak to him? It was the day we celebrated Ramadan, the end of it … And I didn't even speak much, I passed my sister-in-law to him and then I regretted it. I haven't spoken to him since.

It's been three months, more than three months, since I've had news from him. I'm constantly running films in my head. Is he dead? Is he alive? Will I be able to live if he dies?

I lost my nephew over there, he left a few days after him.

Samira

I said: right. I said: since she doesn't understand that I want you back, I said: right, I have to go there. It was my destiny to go. She has an image of a mum at home, a mum who works and everything. She thinks: Yes, my mum would never dare leave a country and go all the way over there. I wanted to show her: my child, wherever you are, if it is the end of the earth, if there is a war or whatever, I will look for you. I will abandon everything, I will come and get you.

And that's what I did in March 2014. I said to the whole world [on the Internet], I said: listen, if you have heard anything about my daughter, or if you know where she is, tell her I will be in Turkey 10 days. Tell her I'll be there. And I went all the way to Kilis to the Syrian border. But they wouldn't let us through. They said ... that because I was a Belgian citizen, that my life would be in too much danger ... But she knew that I came and to prove to her I said: See, look. I see all these Syrian people at the border who want to go home, but there's a war. They have fled from there and you are going there. I said: look how the world has turned upside down.

When my daughter, it's strange to say, I didn't know the Syrians. Because she left to go to that country, I thought badly of them. I thought: Yeah, I don't like them. And [then] when I went over there and I met these people there at the border, this mass of people who were also suffering, who were dying there, and who had families, who had left their lives behind as well, so I said: Oh my, I thought I had probl ... come on. And they, Even they wanted to protect me. Because they had already heard about the State and all of that. They said: oh, be careful, they'll cut you up.

I wanted to see my daughter, that's all. That was my battle and it's still going on – and I'm not giving up – I think I would like to go back there again. I said to myself ... I said that maybe if she sees me, if they let me see her and that she sees me ... at the last minute she will leave with me.

The next time, I will say to her, come on, that we miss her, that I love her.

Yasmin

Now, even if we go somewhere, to a restaurant *(long pause she cries)* it's not the same. In March it was my son, who's 23, birthday. He wanted to to go a restaurant with the whole family and everything. We were all there but there was something missing. Karim wasn't there. That was very very hard to take in.

We need to learn to live with it, but it's very very very very very hard.

Geraldine

I know that at the end, before he died, my son had left the IS group he was in because he didn't want to do what he was being asked to do but you can't leave the group when you want to over there. And so they tried to get him back, and in getting him back he was wounded in the leg because they actually shot at him. He wasn't able to walk or anything for two or three months. And so I know that they wanted to make him do things that he didn't want to do. For sure several times, he called me to tell me: Mum, if I ever want to come back, will you pay for my plane ticket? I said: yes, I'll pay, of course. And erh ... and then 4 hours later, he would phone me: no, no, forget what I said. I'm staying with my brothers here. I'm not coming home.

My son died in February 2015. He died on the 23rd. I only found out on the 26th. I found out via a message I received from a friend of his who was over there, who said to me: Are you Anis's mother? I said: yes, yes, I'm Anis's mum. Well, I would like to tell you that your son died sometime in the night between Monday and Tuesday, during the US attack on Deir Ezzor airport. So there was an attack, because they wanted to take back the airport, which was in the hands of Islamic State and so he died during it. But you should be proud of your son, he was a lion, many people are sad that he is dead and everything.

I don't have anything, no documents, no photos, I don't have anything you see. And I asked lots of times where he was buried ... *(long pause, she's crying)* and they told me his grave was next to the airport, but there's nothing there I mean, so it's just a grave, there's nothing there.

Yasmin

My children are, are everything to me. Even though I have 4, I feel like I've lost everything. It's not kind to the others, but I've lost everything. I got it wrong, I got my job as a mother wrong. Even though people tell me that's not true I know I got it wrong. Because if he'd had what he was looking for ... here at home ... I have photos that he's sent me, he's happy over there. He has a happy face. And when I compare them to photos from before he left, he didn't look comfortable in his own skin. I mean instead of feeling at home here, he didn't feel it, he found [happiness] in a country at war. *(She's still crying.)* Why? *(Long pause.)* Perhaps that's why I blame myself so much.

Geraldine

On the Tuesday, the day after his death, but I didn't know that he was dead, I had a really bad headache. But I never get headaches, and I thought it was strange.

And in fact I found out that my son died from a bullet in the head. And I told myself: well, it was probably a sign from him. *(She cries.)*

I got a message from the person in charge of all the young Belgians out ... who said to me: Madam, your son still had $400, shall I send it to you? I said: no, don't send those $400. Use them, give them to a Syrian family, but do something good with it. Then he said to me: yes, but no, the Syrians agree with democracy, Syrians don't like us. I said: well do whatever you want with the $400 but do something good whatever you do. That's all I can say to you.

Samira

What also terrifies me, what I have nightmares about, if one day *(speaks Arabic)* if I phone her back, the word that I want ... it's sad to say it but it haunts me ... I am frightened because when you fall over, or something happens to you, even when you're grown-up, the first thing you say is: Mama.

Mama, Mama. When we're afraid. *(She shouts.)* Mama! And that's what I'm frightened of ... *(Pause.)* If she calls for me, it's her last word, and I don't even hear it.

Geraldine

I went to the Syrian border, so to Kilis in Turkey, where it's really the gateway to get to Aleppo, and I went out there with my son's clothes in fact. And over there, you've got all the Syrian families who are trying to get back to Syria, and I gave my son's clothes to a mother who also had a boy and I said to her: here, my son wanted to help you *(she cries)*, and with his clothes in fact, it's a second chance for him to help. And the mum says to me: but how can you do this? I said: yes, because my son wanted to help the Syrians so I am helping you too. And I had a little bit of money and I gave it to her because she was going through some tests because she was ill and she said to me: no, you shouldn't. I said: Yes I should, because it's my son's money and this way my son is still helping you. *(She cries.)* And the mum was pregnant in fact and she said to me: what was your son called? I said: well, his name was Anis. She said to me: my son, I'll call him Anis. *(She cries.)* So *inshallah,* now there's a mother whose son is called Anis.

There, that's the mum's story.

By the same author

Guantanamo – Honour Bound to Defend Freedom
9781840024746

The Riots
9781849431996

WWW.OBERONBOOKS.COM

Follow us on www.twitter.com/@oberonbooks
& www.facebook.com/OberonBooksLondon

.

Lightning Source UK Ltd.
Milton Keynes UK
UKHW020628170122
397262UK00006B/186